LES ZIAUX [EYESEAS]

Raymond Queneau. Paris, 1973.

RAYMOND QUENEAU

LES ZIAUX [EYESEAS]

TRANSLATED
WITH AN INTRODUCTION
by
DANIELA HUREZANU &
STEPHEN KESSLER

BOSTON, MASS.

LES ZIAUX (EYESEAS) BY RAYMOND QUENEAU

Black Widow Press edition, July 2008

Black Widow Press is an imprint of Commonwealth Books, Inc., Boston.
Joseph S. Phillips, Publisher.
Distributed throughout North America/Canada/UK by NBN (National Book Network)

All Black Widow Press books are printed on acid-free paper and put into sewn and glued bindings. Black Widow Press and its logo are registered trademarks of Commonwealth Books, Inc.

Black Widow Press
www.blackwidowpress.com

Library of Congress Cataloging-in-Publication Data

Queneau, Raymond, 1903-1976.
[Ziaux. English & French]
Les ziaux = Eyeseas / Raymond Queneau ; translated with an introduction by Daniela Hurezanu & Stephen Kessler.
p. cm.
ISBN 978-0-9795137-4-9 (alk. paper)
I. Hurezanu, Daniela. II. Kessler, Stephen, 1947- III. Title. IV. Title: Eyeseas.

PQ2633.U43Z313 2008
841'.912--dc22

2008023407

Prepress production by Windhaven Press (www.windhaven.com)
Printed by Friesens
Printed in Canada

10 9 8 7 6 5 4 3 2 1

CONTENTS

Acknowledgments

Some of the translations in this book first appeared in the following publications: "Shadow": *New Orleans Review;* "Iris" & "ING": *Absinthe*; "Seahorses": *Circumference*; "The Water Tanks," "It's Raining," "Materia Garrulans," "[Misery of My Life]": *Exquisite Corpse*; "[Days have gone by]," "[Light chases]," "[The Shadow reveals]," "[Such a wise]," "[The Half-baked sermon]": *Action Yes*; "Ideas": *Field*; "Swan-Signs," "Black Magic," "White Magic," "Crevasse," "Eyeseas" (under the title "Eyewaters"): *Translation—A Translation Studies Journal*; "From the Desert," "[Deaf]," "The Explanation of Metaphors": *Poetic Voices without Borders* (anthology, Gival Press, 2008); "Robinson," "The Shipwreck," "Clock," "Recent Aspects of the Middle Ages," "The Outskirts": *Sulphur River Literary Review*; "Vigil," "Harbor," "The Dogs of Asnières," "Calm is the Tree": *Zoland Poetry* (anthology, Steerforth Press, 2007); "[Everything's raw]": *Cairn*.

Translators' Preface

In the United States, Raymond Queneau is known mainly for his novel *Zazie dans le métro,* which was made into a film by Louis Malle, for *Exercises in Style,* translated by Barbara Wright, and for being the founder and one of the most important members of the literary movement known as *Oulipo*. Yet, in spite of an increased interest in *Oulipo* and its esthetics, very few people actually *read* Queneau. One of the reasons for this paradoxical situation is the fact that he is virtually impossible to translate. The essence of his writings resides not in its "content," but in the sounds and the form of the text—to be faithful to the form, a translator must often violate the content, and vice-versa.

Queneau was born in 1903 in the provincial town of Le Havre and moved to Paris in 1920, where he studied philosophy at the Sorbonne and became involved in the Dadaist movement. Between 1924 and 1929 he was one of the most active members of the Surrealist circle, and married Janine Kahn, the sister of André Breton's first wife. During this period he co-authored several Surrealist pamphlets and contributed short texts to *La Révolution Surréaliste*, the official magazine of the movement. But like other members of the group, he grew disenchanted with Breton, mostly for personal reasons, and in 1930—together with Georges Bataille, Michel Leiris, Roger Vitrac and several others—he produced *Un Cadavre*, an incendiary pamphlet directed against Breton.

After breaking with the Surrealists, Queneau began to devote more time to his other passions: painting, mathematics and philosophy. In 1933 his first novel, *Le Chiendent*, came out, and from then on he published almost every year another novel or a collection of poetry. Beyond these numerous and various intellectual interests, Queneau was very aware of the public sphere and maintained throughout his life, in a Europe that was to be ravaged by both National Socialism and Stalinism, a rare lucidity. In 1932 he joined the anti-Stalinist movement and the *Front Commun* against fascism. During the war he engaged in various activities meant to help the French Resistance and refused to write for any of the publications supporting the new regime.

After the war, while continuing to write fiction and poetry, he found yet another means of expression: film. He founded a film company with Boris Vian and Michel Arnaud, collaborated briefly with Luis Buñuel and Alain Resnais, and even played a role in Claude Chabrol's *Landru*. Public recognition for his literary work came in 1951 when he was elected a member of the jury of the renowned Académie Goncourt.

The final chapter in Queneau's life unfolded from 1960, when *Oulipo* was launched, until his death in 1976. This *Ouvroir de Littérature Potentielle*, founded in collaboration with François Le Lionnais, carried forward many of the literary values championed by Queneau in his youth. For Queneau, *Oulipo* was a *quest* whose main characteristics were naiveté, craftiness and fun—the latter invoked in reelation to what he called "fun mathematics." Through constrained writing techniques and mathematical models applied to the realm of literature, *Oulipo* members created some of the most innovative twentieth-century works, such as Georges Perec's *La Disparation/A Void* or Queneau's *Cent mille milliards de poèmes*.

Les Ziaux includes poems written from 1920 to 1943 and is divided into four sections, each revealing a different side of Queneau's sensibility and different tones of voice. The first part is light, playful, almost naïve, with poems whose composition is informed by such banal events as the death of a fly. But the playful tone doesn't exclude gravity, and even through these poems the reader can feel the grim presence of death, as in "Under the

Roofs"/"Sous les Toits" and "Seahorses"/"Hippocampes," which starts in the usual light tone and ends by evoking the image of a corpse. Then there are the very formal poems, written in rhymed *alexandrin*, the twelve-syllable classical French line, which presents tricky problems for translators. We chose to replace the *alexandrin* with a roughly iambic pentameter line, and although we tried to honor end rhyme, we didn't make a fetish of it; we focused rather on finding approximations of Queneau's frequent use of assonance, consonance and alliteration, and tried to stick as closely as possible to the spirit of the poem.

The second section includes some of the book's funniest poems: "The Ridiculous Meal/Le Repas Ridicule," "Loozing Wait/Maigrir," "The Grandfather Clock"/"La Pendule"—poems written in a colloquial idiom often reproduced phonetically and brimming with dark humor. It also includes a poem written in the tradition of Surrealist free association, "Materia Garrulans," and "It's Raining"/Il pleut," a poem that anticipates a technique evident in the last section of the book where words are hybridized into Queneauesque combinations ("shower" and "umbrella" into "showerella," "eyes" and "waters" into "eyewaters"—which we render as "eyeseas").

Another poem using mathematical combinations, "Don Evané Marquy," which we translated as "Don Evans Margy," is practically untranslatable, if by "translating" one means translating the "meaning." Since translators are always faced with a choice, the most faithful choice we could make here was to re-create the poem according to its underlying esthetics, that is, the fact that each line is an anagram of the title. In doing so, it was impossible to also translate the meaning of the words, but since the lines of the original are themselves nonsensical, we believe we didn't betray the spirit of the poem. Our translation is faithful to its mathematical combinations, its irreverence and playfulness; our anagrams aren't "perfect," but then, neither are Queneau's. And we were even able to realize something he unsuccessfully tried: to create new words on the vertical formed by each line's first letter ("Gey My Ass").

The third part is, in some respects, the most contemporary in its style, its self-consciousness and its imagery. The poems in this section—or the one long poem—are untitled and revolve around the theme of death, of time going by and of a melancholy autumnal nature evoking a sense of existential despair. A common technique he uses here is the repetition of a word, which gives the poem, freed from the conventions of traditional versification—although rhyme is not entirely absent—a more seductive musicality.

The fourth part is probably the most interesting stylistically. From the *ars poetica* expressed in "The Explanation of Metaphors"/"L'Explication des métaphores" to "Eyeseas"/"Les Ziaux," which closes the volume, the poems are in four-line stanzas with end rhymes, yet they are not "traditional." Following a poetic intuition he would later develop in *Oulipo*, Queneau keeps inventing rules for himself that force him to write a poem within a given framework. It is of course practically impossible to follow all these rules in the English translation and at the same time create something as linguistically convincing as the original. So we focused on creating a *poem* first of all, and tried to respect the rules laid out by Queneau only insofar as the essence of the poem was determined by them. For example, in translating "Black Magic"/"Magie noire" and "White Magic"/"Magie blanche," we kept the structure of the sonnet and invented English words modeled on Queneau's neologisms, most of them based on phonetic associations. We were able to replicate the form of "White Magic" whose lines start with the same letter within each stanza, but it was impossible to obey this rule in translating "Black Magic"—as a matter of fact, Queneau himself is unable to do it; there are a few letters that keep "getting out of line."

In translating "Les Ziaux"—probably the most beautiful poem in this collection—we faced not only the challenge of inventing hybridized words—"eyeseas"—but the task of translating Queneau's subversion of grammar. In French, "les eaux" is feminine and "les yeux" is masculine, but Queneau uses the masculine for all the adjectives modifying "les eaux," and the feminine for those modifying "les yeux." Considering the fact that objects don't have a gender in English, this was, of course, impossible to replicate, and we had to focus on creating a similar effect by using the possibilities of the English language.

Eyeseas is representative of Queneau's range of poetic voices. We hope this translation will not only fill a serious void but may also help to inspire interest in the work of one of the most important French writers of the twentieth century.

—DH & SK

LES ZIAUX

(1920–1943)

I

PORT

Le mur qui s'allonge
et le toit qui plonge
les bois tout pourris
ne sont plus ici

La grue très oblique
les porcs les barriques
bien que disparus
sont rien moins que vus

Ce bateau sans grâce
près du ciel s'efface
laissant le jour gris
s'enfuir avec lui

Le Havre, 1920.

HARBOR

The lengthening wall
the roofs as they fall
the wood all rotten
are all but forgotten

The dangling rigs
the barrels the pigs
gone as they are
aren't really so far

This ship without grace
disappears in space
unmoored the gray day
sails slowly away

SOUS LES TOITS

La mouche est morte au clair de lune
sur un vieux journal empaillé
je suis heureux de ma fortune:
dans huit jours la mansarde à louer

Les coteaux se sculptent dans l'ombre
les toits réverbèrent la nuit
une radio sur un air sombre
seule fait entendre son bruit

La mouche est morte au clair de lune
sur un vieux journal empaillé
je suis heureux de ma fortune:
dans huit jours la mansarde à louer

UNDER THE ROOFS

The fly is dead under the moon
on an old newspaper crumpled up
I'm happy enough with my good luck:
eight days and I can rent my room

Shadows sculpt the shape of hills
the roofs reverberate the night
a radio plays a tune that spills
its sadness as the only sound

The fly is dead under the moon
on an old newspaper crumpled up
I'm happy enough with my good luck:
eight days and I can rent my room

HIPPOCAMPES

Hippocampes verts
nageurs singuliers
vous avez peuplé
mes rêves d'hiver

Autant préférer
Pégase! Licorne!
pou d'ivoire gris
qui trotte paisible

Le passant s'enfuit
loin du réverbère
sous lequel enfoui
un mort désespère

SEAHORSES

Green seahorses
singular swimmers
you have filled
my winter dreams

So much for preferring
Pegasus! Licorn!
gray ivory lice
routinely trotting

The passerby flees
the streetlamp's light
beneath which is buried
a hopeless corpse

ASPECTS RÉCENTS DU MOYEN AGE

Plus purs que ne furent les roses
qu'apportèrent les Paladins
des valets dont nul ne dispose
préparent d'étonnants festins
aux Rois aux Reines et aux Nombres
cinquante-deux serfs du destin

Le feu du sol qui se révèle
par la froideur des étincelles
de ces lames d'or et d'argent
tisse de métal et de laine
un étendard se transformant
en un torchon sali de haine

Les rues désertes accomplissent
la réalité des chemins
le ciel flambe pour que rougissent
les physionomies sans destin
attendant l'heure qui approche
de l'ombre que jette une main

RECENT ASPECTS OF THE MIDDLE AGES

Purer than ancient roses
brought in by valiant Knights
courtiers in royal poses
prepare extravagant nights
for Kings for Queens and for the Numbers
fifty-two servants of the heights

The ground's deep fire flares high
in sprays of cold sparks that flash
like blades of gold and silver swords
woven of metal and of wool
a flag transformed as if by fate
to a rag filthy with hate

The empty streets fulfill
the roads' reality
a fiery sky that reddens
faces with no destiny
just waiting for the time
of the shadowy hand to be

L'AMPHION

Le Paris que vous aimâtes
n'est pas celui que nous aimons
et nous nous dirigeons sans hâte
vers celui que nous oublierons

Topographies! itinéraires!
dérives à travers la ville!
souvenirs des anciens horaires!
que la mémoire est difficile . . .

Et sans un plan sous les yeux
on ne nous comprendra plus
car tout ceci n'est que jeu
et l'oubli d'un temps perdu

AMPHION

The Paris you once loved
isn't the same today
and the one with us now
will soon be yesterday

Topographies! Itineraries!
rambles around the town!
old agendas remembered!
the memory brings me down . . .

Without a map in front of them
they'll never understand why
for this is nothing but a game
forgetting of a time gone by

VILLE ÉTRANGÈRE

I

Terrassé par les habitudes
de maux qui tentent d'aboutir
le pauvre dans sa solitude
attend le moment de partir

pour des cieux des mers ou des terres
où nul ne voudrait asservir
l'inquiétude d'un esprit fier
à la honte d'un repentir

FOREIGN CITY

I

Crushed by the endless
chain of all things evil
the poor man in his aloneness
waits for the chance to leave

for skies seas or lands
where no one would think to enslave
a restless mind too proud
to be contrite or ashamed

II

Plaies des matinées sans travail
l'hiver est fait de trahisons
le long des rues lorsque l'on bâille
adossé contre une maison
comme le pauvre qui travaille
à continuer les pâmoisons
de ces chaussures qui trop bâillent
et des bouches sans oraisons

II

Wounded workless mornings
winter is made of betrayals
along streets where you yawn
leaning against a house
like a poor man who labors
to revive the faint breaths
of these yawning shoes
and of these mouths without a prayer

III

Seul souvenir des temps passés
un jour d'hiver qui agonise
irez-vous pauvres trépassés
corrompre la mer qui se brise
sur les falaises échancrées
ou bien glacés par vents et brises
gémir tout le long de l'année
sur un malheur qui s'éternise?

III

The sole memento of time gone by
one dying winter day
will you poor dead go on
tainting the breaking waves
that smash against the cliffs
or frozen by the winds
will you moan all year long
through an eternity of misery?

IV

L'obscurité des loups qui meurent de misère
les faubourgs sont trop loin pour la clarté des jours

IV

The wolves in darkness dying of starvation
the town's edge just beyond the light of day

V

L'année blanche des jours qui se sont écoulés
attend avec passion une fin trop commune
le pauvre qui la suit regarde dérailler
les désespoirs communs d'une plèbe importune
ô temps déjà passés n'avez-vous point failli
dégager les malheurs des peines trop communes?
mais les jours se sont tus tout le long de l'année
la neige des hivers termine sa ceinture
et le pauvre qui suit regarde s'évanouir
les espoirs unissant cette plèbe importune

V

The white year of days that won't return
eagerly awaits an all too common end
the poor man watching the hopeless mob
sees its despair go off the rails
oh yesterdays have you not failed
to release the misery from common pains?
but the days have gone silent the whole long year
the winter snow has sealed the earth
and the poor man following sees the hope
that kept the mob together disappear

VI

Vaisseaux indifférents qui présidez au sort
des incertains bandits poursuivant la fortune
transportez mes destins et ma vie importune
au-delà des baisers du bonheur qui s'endort

Londres, 1922.

VI

You indifferent ships presiding over the fate
of slippery bandits running after riches
carry my future and my wretched state
away beyond the luck of dozing kisses

London, 1922

IDÉES

Les oiseaux bleus dans l'air sont verts dans la prairie
qui les entend les voit qui les voit les entend
leur aile déployée élargit leur patrie
mais à travers leur plume un feu toujours s'étend

Caméléons du ciel agiles que l'œil transperce
nuages qui vivants assument tour à tour
la forme d'une idée et puis l'idée adverse
protéens dont l'azur ne limite aucun tour

Ils volent à travers la sublime excellence
des principes divins scellés sur l'horizon
les étoiles parfois dénotent leur présence
et les jeux de la lune au cours d'une saison

IDEAS

Blue birds above are green when on the ground
heard they are seen and seen they're also heard
their wings extend the borders of their land
but from their feathers winged fires spread

Clouds come alive in various changing forms
agile chameleons seen by the sharpened eye
ideas and then their opposites in turn
protean in the limitless blue sky

They're sailing through the purest excellence
of sublime laws stamped into the horizon
the stars may make the moon's games and their own
visibly present in the course of a season

IRIS

Ces longs ponts traversant les cieux brillent de gloire
et sacrifient leur arche aux multiples couleurs
le vert gémit parfois le bleu dans sa douleur
saigne comme un vrai dieu auquel il nous faut croire

Suivant un cours certain à travers les étoiles
jaillit le lait béni qui fonda la blancheur
trouée ainsi la nuit laisse couler sans voiles
le galion incertain de l'angoisse et des pleurs

Nul ne triomphera dans cette cavalcade
ô Théâtre du Monde illustré par l'horreur
toute teinte exsudée ondule et devient fade
quand le sel a perdu sa violente fraîcheur

Les siècles ont transmis l'énigme et la sagesse
les longs ponts dessinaient leurs sûres trajectoires
au plan de la nature en joie et en détresse
échos sans volontés très fidèles miroirs

IRIS

These bridges across the sky shine in their splendor
and sacrifice their arc to countless colors
green moans at times and blue in its own pain
bleeds like a god whose truth we can't deny

Along the well worn path among the stars
springs the sacred milk of the first whiteness
and so through its wound the night lets flow
the galleon of tears and anguish blown off course

No one will triumph in this cavalcade
oh Theater of the World that mirrors horror
all shades exuded undulate then fade
when salt has lost the violence of its power

The centuries sent forth mystery and wisdom
long bridges showed their sure trajectories
following nature's plan in joys and sorrows
echoes adrift these ever faithful mirrors

VEILLE

Si les feux dans la nuit faisaient des signes certes
la peur serait un rire et l'angoisse un pardon
mais les feux dans la nuit sans cesse déconcertent
le guetteur affiné par la veille et le froid

VIGIL

If the lights in the night made explicit signs
fear would be laughter and anguish forgiveness
but for the guard on edge in the cold
the lights in the night are unsettling lines

ROBINSON

Sur la mer morte auprès des feux couchants
La sirène aux arbres déracinés qui flottent
A donné l'ombre de ses seins et de ses reins
Les claques de la vague paraissent aux noyés
L'indice des poissons accourus noctivagues
Lorsque fuient l'eau salée la coque les pieux de fer
Les mâts chargés de fleurs et les nuages exsangues
S'abattant sur la grève où vient dormir l'été
Aimantés par la mort les astrolabes les planches
Et les cerceaux de rhum roulent jusqu'à la falaise
Auprès des tables sales et des verres mal lavés
L'épice des cafés dans la plaine étonnée
Ne reflète aucun lion rampant dans cette nuée
Banalement vêtu de soie de pourpre et d'or
Les forêts ont perdu le sourire des herbes
Et les bergers mordillent leurs sifflets de sureau
Touristes assidus peintres et demoiselles
Abandonnent la ville où l'on ne chante plus
Depuis que l'assassin a perdu ses bretelles
Dans les cachots de plomb où nul ne s'est pendu.

ROBINSON

On the dead sea alongside the sunset
The siren has given to the rootless floating
Trees the shadow of her breasts and waist
To those that drowned the sound of waves
Is like fish slipping thru the nightswells
When the hull the iron spikes reject the salty water
The flowery mast and ashen clouds
Invading the beach where the astrolabes
Drawn by death come to sleep in summer
The wooden planks and rum barrels roll down
To the cliffs near dirty tables and unwashed glasses
The coffee spice across the plain in wonder
Reflects no lion strolling in this haze
Wearing the usual silk purple and gold
The forests have lost their leafy smile
And shepherds bite their elderwood flutes
Assiduous tourists young girls and painters
Have fled the city where nobody sings anymore
Since the assassin lost his suspenders
In the dark cells where no one hanged himself.

LE NAUFRAGE

Les cristaux dans la ruche ont fait mauvais ménage
Négligeant les patins des traqueurs de cerceaux
Et la nuit où surgit cet étrange carnage
Une algue serpentait en de mouvants arceaux

Afin de ne donner aux porteurs d'arbalète
Que les fruits obsédés par la pâleur d'un sein
Une femme empruntait au peintre sa palette
Et chantait le décès d'un poète assassin

Qu'importe les passions de ces nuits aberrantes
Et les appels d'Ulysse aux sirènes errantes
Si l'écluse des cieux se ferme pour toujours

Et qu'importe l'ennui qui surprend les rameurs
Si les flots de la neige emportent les clameurs
Des cavernes flottant dans la clarté des jours.

THE SHIPWRECK

The crystals in the hive weren't getting along
Neglecting the treasure hunters' search for wrecks
And in the night of this strange butchery
A rope of seaweed circled restlessly

In order to give the archers just the fruit
Tormented by the whiteness of a breast
A woman took a painter's palette's colors
And sang a murderer poet's lyric death

Who cares about the passions of these wild nights
And Ulysses' calls to the wandering sirens
If the skies' locks remain forever shut

And who cares about the boredom of the crew
If waves of snow are carrying off the sound
Of caverns floating in the day's bright blue.

ON

On allume la lampe derrière les bocaux
On ne vient pas sonner pour l'insomnie
Mais autour des maisons du centre ville
On effiloche des ombres d'ombres
Dans les fils de l'étoile on accroche des mannequins
Pensées mortes avaries et cancres
Les tuiles du destin tombent en chantonnant
Sur la gueule infiniment longue des passants
Des refrains enchaînent les hommes
A leurs goûts putréfiés
On plante des palissades
Que des yeux rouges gardent.

ING

Behind the jars the light is coming on
Nobody's ringing insomnia's bells
But all around the houses in the town
Somebody's shredding shadows of shadows
Manikins are hanging from the strings of stars
Dead thoughts damages and dunces
Destiny's tiles are dropping like songs
Into the gaping mouths of passersby
Tunes are shackling men
To their rotting taste
Long walls are getting planted
Red eyes are keeping watch.

GRANDE BANLIEUE

Sur le paysage lent qui s'accroît sans cesse
des herbes et des fruits qui mûrissent l'été
la nature bonne princesse
lance l'alouette de la liberté

Dans les jardins cachés où ne se révèle
pas l'histoire des ombres effacées
l'eau fourmille en ses voiles
de mercure et d'argent froissés

A son heure l'aube opportune
fait cesser l'asthme et l'insomnie
les crabes courent sur la lune
qui près de l'étoile frémit

La mer n'est qu'une opale verte
loin d'elle un marin endormi
calme ses os endoloris
et rêve de découvertes

THE OUTSKIRTS

In the slow landscape ceaselessly spreading
from grass and summer's ripening fruit
princess nature in her goodness
launches freedom's lark

In hidden gardens where the history
of rubbed-out shadows is never revealed
water sparkles in its veils
of shimmering mercury and silver

Just in time the sun comes up
to relieve asthma and insomnia
crabs are crawling across the moon
which trembles next to its star

The sea is nothing more than a green opal
far in the distance a sailor sleeps
his aching bones are calm
and he is dreaming of discoveries

TULÉ

Atteint d'une flèche au cœur
le vieux roi s'écroule en pleurant
Gérard le console
Son front pur s'incline
Il penche la tête
Un archer murmure
c'est un révolté
Des gendarmes arrivent
Gérard Gérard pourquoi n'empêcheras-tu pas cette
coupe
d'aller rejoindre sous l'Océan
les trésors phosphorescents
couverts d'infusoires et de radiolaires
On t'emmène au poste de police
Ton double seul en sortira

THULE

Struck by an arrow to the heart
the old king collapses sobbing
Gérard consoles him
His head tilts forward
He nods
An archer whispers
"He's a rebel"
The gendarmes arrive
Gérard Gérard can't you keep this goblet
from joining the phosphorescent treasures
covered with infusers and radiolairs
under the Ocean
They take you to the police station
Only your double will get out

L'HORLOGE

Horloge mince comme le temps
horloge couleur de jonquille
ton cadran flotte sur le mur
incertaine dérivation
la petite roue s'isole et ne cesse de chanter
elle sépare deux hommes assis qui pleurent
coiffés d'une balance
condamnés à cette dérision
(c'est moi-même et moi-même encore)
spirale de la vie receleur du ciel
jaguar prêt à bondir
le balancier s'enroule autour de la sphère des heures
justes trépidations sévères commandements

THE CLOCK

Clock as thin as time
clock yellow as a daffodil
your screen floats on the wall
from who knows where
the little wheel pops out and won't stop singing
it jumps between two seated weeping men
a scale on their heads
condemned to this mockery
(it is myself and myself again)
spiral of life catching the sky
jaguar set to spring
the pendulum encircles the sphere of hours
true trepidations hard commandments

A PARTIR DU DÉSERT

à partir du désert
à partir des fleurs qui ne croissent pas
où passe le signe de la lumière
entre les herbes salées
les squelettes qui nagent

à partir du désert
qui veut la ligne des horizons
trente mille horizons
trente mille points d'eau

à partir du désert
la caravane oscille lentement
à droite à gauche
tout vient d'un coup
plus rien derrière les dunes

à partir du désert le feu qui transforme
diversité de la dernière oasis
trente mille palmiers
trente mille points d'eau

à partir du désert
on prend sa route
à partir des oasis diverses
vers l'unité de trente mille horizons
vers le feu qui transforme
le ciel
la terre

FROM THE DESERT

from the desert
from the ungrowing flowers
where the light's sign slips by
between salty grasses
and swimming skeletons

from the desert
reaching for the horizons
thirty thousand horizons
thirty thousand watering holes

from the desert
the caravan moves slowly
to the right to the left
everything comes at once
nothing behind the dunes

from the desert the transforming fire
variousness of the last oasis
thirty thousand palms
thirty thousand watering holes

from the desert
we take its road
from various oases
toward the oneness of thirty thousand horizons
toward the fire transforming
the sky
the earth

LES CITERNES

Au milieu des terrains désertés
parmi la suie des soies brûlées
auprès de la bourse des valeurs
non loin des piliers du crépuscule
sous le cadran des équinoxes
par delà les gelées blanches du temps
au fond de l'œil des quatre coins
au centre du métropolitain
il y a les citernes

THE WATER TANKS

In the middle of deserted lots
amidst the soot of the burnt silks
not far from the stock market
close to the pillars of sundown
under the screen of the equinoxes
beyond the white frost of time
deep in the eye of the four corners
in the center of the subway
        that's where the water tanks are

II

LE REPAS RIDICULE

Une fois n'est pas coutume: allons au restaurant
nous payer du caviar et des ptits' ortolans

Consultons le journal à la rubrique esbrouffe
révélant le bon coin où pour pas cher on bouffe

Nous irons à çui-ci, nous irons à çui-là
mais y a des objections: l'un aimm ci, l'autre aimm ça

Je propose: engouffrons notre appétit peu mince
au bistrot le troisième après la rue Huyghens

Tous d'accord remontons le boulevard Raspail
jusqu'aux bars où l'on suss la mouss avec des pailles

Hans William Vladimir et Jean-Jacques Dupont
avalent goulûment de la bière en ballon

Avec ces chers amis d'un pas moins assuré
nous trouverons enfin le ptit endroit rêvé

Les couteaux y sont mous les nappes y sont sales
la serveuse sans fards parfume toutt la salle

Le patron—un gourmet! vous fait prendre—c'est fou!
du pipi pour du vin et pour du foi' du mou

La patronne a du cran et rince les sardines
avec une huile qui fut huile dparaffine

THE RIDICULOUS MEAL

It wouldn't hurt one time: let's go to a restaurant
To get some caviar and a bit of ortolan

Let's check the paper for the trendy places
where we can strut in and stuff our faces

Between one and the other we can't decide
I like this, I like that, we all take sides

Here's what I say: let's go whole hog
in the third joint from Huyghens down the block

Up on Raspail we cruise the bars
where the customers sip their suds thru straws

Jean-Jacques Dupont and Hans William Vladimir
chugalug pitchers and mugs of beer

Me and my buddies stagger down the street
till we find the spot where we wanted to eat

The knives are dull, the tables a mess
the ugly waitress stinks up the place

The owner—a gourmet! Serves up—it's nuts!
piss in wineglasses and shit on the plates

His wife has the gall to rinse the sardines
with oil that's recycled kerosene

La carne nous amène un rôti d'aspect dur
orné concentricment de légumes impurs

Elle proposera les miettes gluantes
d'une tête de veau que connurent les lentes

Elle proposera les panards englués
d'un porc qui négligea toujours de les laver

Peut-être qu'un produit à l'état naturel
échappra-z-aux méfaits dla putréfiantt femelle

« Voici ma belle enfant un petit nerf de bœuf
que vous utilizrez pour casser tous vos œufs »

De l'omelette jaune où nage le persil
elle fera-z-hélas un morceau d'anthraci

Ce bon charbon croquant bien craquant sous la dent
se blanchira d'un sel sous la dent bien crissant

Plutôt que de noircir un intestin qui grêle
nous dévorerons la simili-porcelaine

L'hôtesse nous voyant grignoter son ménage
écaillera les murs de l'ampleur de sa rage

Alors avalerons fourchettes et couteaux
avant d'avec vitesse enfiler nos manteaux

Fuyards nous galoprons dans la rue où ça neige
sans peur de déchirer la couturr de nos grèges

The bitch brings out a gross hunk of meat
surrounded by greens too disgusting to eat

She dares to recommend the rotting head
of a lice-ridden calf that's long since dead

Then she suggests the feet of a hog
that never got washed its whole life long

Maybe some food in its natural form
will escape this revolting woman's harm

"Here you go, honey, a nice beef bone
for beating your eggs to a frothy foam"

She turns a yellow omelet with parsley garnish
to a lump of coal with a coat of varnish

This good crisp charcoal will whiten your teeth
like rock salt cracking the bones of your cheek

Instead of increasing the pain in our guts
we'd be better off chewing on the plastic plates

Seeing us eating her best tableware
the hostess gets mad and strips the walls bare

Then we scarf down the forks and knives
grab our jackets and run for our lives

We hightail it down the street in the snow
fearless of ripping our pants as we go

Nous retournant au bout de cinquante ou cent mètres
nous verrons le souillon jouer au gazomètre

et nous péter au nez ses infâmes insultes
— patronne de bistrot, empoisonneuse occulte

We turn around after a hundred yards
and even from here we can smell her farts

And so our hostess has the last laugh
— our noses still smarting from her poison gas

IL PLEUT

Averse averse averse averse averse averse
pluie ô pluie ô pluie ô! ô pluie ô pluie ô pluie!
gouttes d'eau gouttes d'eau gouttes d'eau gouttes d'eau
parapluie ô parapluie ô paraverse ô!
paragouttes d'eau paragouttes d'eau de pluie
capuchons pèlerines et imperméables
que la pluie est humide et que l'eau mouille et mouille!
mouille l'eau mouille l'eau mouille l'eau mouille l'eau
et que c'est agréable agréable agréable
d'avoir les pieds mouillés et les cheveux humides
tout humides d'averse et de pluie et de gouttes
d'eau de pluie et d'averse et sans un paragoutte
pour protéger les pieds et les cheveux mouillés
qui ne vont plus friser qui ne vont plus friser
à cause de l'averse à cause de la pluie
à cause de l'averse et des gouttes de pluie
des gouttes d'eau de pluie et des gouttes d'averse
cheveux désarçonnés cheveux sans parapluie

IT'S RAINING

Shower shower shower shower shower shower
rain oh rain oh rain oh! oh rain oh rain oh rain!
waterdrops waterdrops waterdrops waterdrops
umbrella oh umbrella oh showerella oh!
waterumbdrops waterdropbrella
hoods capes and raincoats
the rain's so wet and the water soaks and soaks!
wet water wet water wet water wet water
and how nice nice nice it is isn't it
to have your feet soaked and your hair all wet
wet from the shower and the rain and the drops
of rainwater and of shower and with no dropbrella
to protect your feet and your wet hair
that won't curl up again won't curl up again
because of the shower because of the rain
because of the shower and the drops of rain
the waterdrops of rain and the showerdrops
unruly hair umbrellaless hair

DON EVANÉ MARQUY

Dyeu n'a monarque
Yva donne marque
Eva n'y marque don
Yve marque d'anon
Qu'y a mon are de nu
Que Yanne a mordu
Ayr eau de mon nu (q!)
Que monde n'y aura

DON EVANS MARGY

God's name vary
Eva's dom granny
Yve's nod gona ram
My naged as(s) manor
Yan'(s) nose gard
As a very mong(k)
Same vayn and morg
So dame angry

UN MILLION DE FAITS

Sur ma table repose un almanach Hachette
de mil neuf cent vingt-deux. Il fallut que j'achète
au prix de quatre francs cet étrange bouquin
que peu souvent on voit vêtu de maroquin
ou de cuir de Russie un jour que la pratique
m'obligeait à connaître un fait de statistique
concernant la culture admise désormais
de l'opium qu'aux Chinois imposent les Anglais
L'ouvrage se présente aux yeux sous une forme
agréable: il n'est point léger non plus qu'énorme
II a plus de deux cents pages in-octavo
et moins de trois cents; on le vend couvert de veau
souple; on le dit impartial et documentaire
son érudition couvre toute la terre
Qui veut savoir comment se nomme du Japon
le ministre des Sports n'a qu'à prendre ce bon
livre afin d'y trouver à la page voulue
le renseignement puis cette phrase étant lue
il pourra reporter sa totale attention
sur le compte rendu qu'on fait de la tension
diplomatique entre URSS et pays balkaniques
dont le sol est truffé de pierres volcaniques
à ce qu'il me semblait. Mais en vain j'ai cherché
la géologie et j'en suis tout dégoûté

A MILLION FACTS

On my table lies a Hachette almanac
from nineteen twenty-two. It cost four francs
to get a copy of this bizarre piece
which not often in Moroccan leather one sees
or in Russian leather one day when the need
forced me a statistical fact to read
regarding the habit of opium smoking
the Chinese picked up from the Brits no joking
The work's a pleasant size and its form is
hardly light but not enormous
with over two hundred pages between
its supple covers of fine calfskin
It's said to be impartial and scholarly
its knowledge covers the earth entirely
If the Japanese Sports minister's name to find
you want, open the book with that in mind
search for the information at the right
page, and only afterwards you might
focus your undivided attention
on the reports of diplomatic tension
between the USSR and the Balkans
where the ground is studded with volcanos
or so it seems to me. But in vain did I look
for geology and, disgusted, I shut the book

MATERIA GARRULANS

la lavande le raisin sec
cure à vos soins mégère truc
accessoire ne dit pas amen
cependant roi fuit d'exil

carnaval rose verbe vierge
sel de roumain verte neige
carnier rude au vert ni sel
à la fin le zouave crie grâce

liberté au témoin naval
civil superbe épaule brune
cœur frappé joue du Natal
le serpent juge un cheval

étoile malabar satin noir
l'heure fermée ni nuit ni jour
le volet mue année pubère
aucune affiche ne chante pouilles

l'hôpital trouble pharmacie
trottoirs en huile de foie de morue
de l'eau de javel pour les gars
de l'iodure pour le municipal

cacahuètes cœur manqué de peu
le jeu d'un mur prêt à se rompre
attire l'œuf d'un chien désossé
carrure faite d'haltères fausses

MATERIA GARRULANS

lavender and raisins too
cure for your cares stuff so shrewd
accessory doesn't say amen
anyway king flees banishment

pink carnival and virgin verb
Romanian salt as green as snow
tough carniver to green nor salt
finally the Zouave cries for help

freedom the sailor witness bears
superb civilian shoulder brown
the wounded heart plays Christmas songs
the snake condemns a guilty horse

stellar stud black satin dude
time never closes day or night
the blinds transform pubescent year
nor any poster chews you out

hospital troubles pharmacy
sidewalks slick with cod liver oil
clorox for the depot floors
iodine dressing City Hall

heart peanuts just out of reach
a wall in play about to fall
attracts an egg's filet of dog
fake weights to build a buffed-out bod

des cravates de dentelle rouge
draguent le fond d'un épi mûr
Nil ou Volga l'as rétamé
cardinaux mis en cuisine

neckties made of reddish lace
drag the bottom of a ripe wheat spike
Nile or Volga washed it out
a dash of bishops in the dish

MAIGRIR

I

Y en a qui maigricent sulla terre
Du vente du coq-six ou des jnous
Y en a qui maigricent le caractère
Y en a qui maigricent pas du tout
        Oui mais
Moi jmégris du bout des douas
Oui du bout des douas Oui du bout des douas
Moi jmégris du bout des douas
Seskilya dplus distinglé

LOOZING WAIT

I

On earth there're guys who looz wait
From their gut and their butt and their 'nees
Some who lose it from their gravitees
Some don't lose any at all
          Yeah but
I looz wait from my fingertips
Yeah my fingertips Yeah my fingertips
I looz wait from my fingertips
The heavliest way of all

II

Lautt jour Boulvar de la Villette
Vlà jrenconte le boeuf à la mode
Jlui dis Tu mas lair un peu blett
Viens que jte paye une belle culotte
Seulement jai pas pu passque
Moi jmégris du bout des douas
Oui du bout des douas Oui du bout des douas
Moi jmégris du bout des douas
Seskilya dplus distinglé

II

On Villette Blvard th'other day
I meet my buddy Beefcake
I tell him Dude you look overdone
C'mon I'll buy you a steak
Only I couldn't do it becuz
I looz wait from my fingertips
Yeah my fingertips Yeah my fingertips
I looz wait from my fingertips
The heavliest way of all

III

Dpuis ctemps-là jfais pus dgymnastique
Et jmastiens des sports dhiver
Et comme avec fureur jmastique
Je pense que si je persévère
        Eh bien
Jmégrirai du bout des douas
Oui du bout des douas Oui du bout des douas
Jmégrirai même de partout
Même de lesstrémité du cou

III

Since then I've stopped workingout
And skip winter sports when it's snowing
And as I chomp my way through life
I think if I can just keep going
Well
I'll looz wait from my fingertips
Yeah my fingertips Yeah my fingertips
I'll even looz wait from everyplace else
like what's at the end of my neck

LA PENDULE

I

Je mballadais sulles boulevards
Lorsque jrencontre lami Bidard
Il avait lair si estomaqué
Que jlui ai dmandé dsesspliquer
        Eh bien voilà me dit-il
Jviens davaler ma pendule
Alors jvais chez lchirurgien
Car jai une peupeur de chien
Que ça mtombe dans les vestibules

THE GRANDFATHER CLOCK

I

I was strolling along the boulevard
When I ran into my friend Bidard
And cause he looked like such a mess
I asked the cause of his distress
        Well then he said
I just swallowed my grandfather clock
So to the surgeon I gotta go
Cause I'm ascascared as shit yaknow
It's gonna fall thru my maledrop

II

Un mois après jrevois mon copain
Il avait lair tout skia dplus rupin
Alors je suis été ltrouver
Et jlavons sommé dsesspliquer
        Eh bien voilà me dit-il
Jgagne ma vie avec ma pendule
Jai su lestomac un petit cadran
Je vends lheure à tous les passants
En attendant qujai lcadran sulles vestibules

II

A month later I run into him again
He looks really fat and happy
So I can't help wondering what's going on
And I ask him what the hell happened
        Well then he said
I make a living with my grandfather clock
There's a little screen on my stomach
And I sell the time to all comers
While I wait for the other shoe to drop

III

A la fin ltype issuissuida
Lossquil eut vu qupersonne lopéra
Et comme jarrivais juste sul chantier
Moi je lui ai demandé qui vienne sesspliquer
Eh bien voilà me dit-il
Jen avais assez davoir une pendule
Ca mempêchait ddormir la nuit
Pour la remonter fallait mfaire un trou dans ldos
Jpréfère être pendu qupendule

III

When nobody'd do the operation
He did himself in in eggsassperation
And as soon as I arrived on the scene
I asked him what does all this mean
Well then he said
I was sick of the tick of that damn clock
It kept me awake night after night
It had to be wound thru a hole in my back
So I hangled up myself on time

IV

Lorsquil fut mort jvais à son enterrement
Cétait lmatin ça mennuyait bien
Mais lorsqui fut dans ltrou ah skon rigola
Quand au fond dla bière le septième coup dmidi tinta
Eh bien voilà voilà voilà
Il avait avalé une pendule
Ca narrive pas à tous les chrétiens
Même à ceux quont un estomm de chien
Et du cœur dans les vestibules

IV

When he died I go to his funeral
Annoyingly early in the ayem
But we had a good laugh as we buried him
And the clock struck noon down in the hole
And so you see and so you see
He'd swallowed the grandfather clock
Which doesn't happen to every soul
Not even to ones with castiron stomachs
And their heart in their maledrop

LES CHIENS D'ASNIÈRES

On enterre les chiens on enterre les chats
on enterre les chevaux on enterre les hommes
on enterre l'espoir on enterre la vie
on enterre l'amour—les amours
on enterre les amours—l'amour
on enterre en silence le silence
on enterre en paix—la paix
la paix—la paix la plus profonde
sous une couche de petits graviers multicolores
de coquilles Saint-Jacques et de fleurs multicolores

il y a une tombe pour tout
à condition d'attendre
il fait nuit il fait jour
à condition d'attendre

la Seine descend vers la mer
l'île immobile ne descend pas
la Seine remontera vers sa source
à condition d'attendre
et l'île naviguera vers le Havre de Grâce
à condition d'attendre

on enterre les chiens on enterre les chats
deux espèces qui ne s'aiment pas

THE DOGS OF ASNIÈRES

Dogs get buried and so do cats
horses get buried and so do men
hope gets buried and so does life
love gets buried—loves
loves get buried—love
silence gets buried in silence
peace gets buried—peace
peace—the deepest peace
under a layer of colorful pebbles
scallops and colorful flowers

there's a grave for everything
if you wait long enough
night falls day dawns
if you wait long enough

the Seine flows down to the sea
the island stays where it is
the Seine will go back to its source
if you wait long enough
and the island will sail toward the Harbor of Grace
if you wait long enough

dogs get buried and so do cats
two species that don't get along

L'HOMME DU TRAMWAY

Cet homme qui marche le long du quai la nuit
le long de la Seine entre Asnières et Courbevoie
cet homme dont l'ombre à chaque instant fuit
suit son chemin droit et sa courbe voie

cet homme a mal aux pieds, misère,
et la fatigue ligote ses épaules
cet homme danse chacun de ses pas
longs comme des nuits d'hiver

depuis une heure le tram ne roule plus
cet homme mesure des kilomètres
à l'épaisseur de ses semelles
il marche la nuit dans cette rue

sa maîtresse l'attend fille peu respectable
elle traîne aux ruisseaux se repaît de bouchers
et son temps se mesure à sa chambre insatiable
qui loge maintenant un homme du tramway

il doit fuir au matin les yeux fort marmiteux
et reprendre la route vers le dépôt sonore
et pendant que la belle dans le pieu dort encore
il soupire qu'il est doux de se sentir aimé

THE STREETCAR MAN

This man walking on the footpath at night
between Asnières and Courbevoie along the Seine
this man whose shadow flickers at each sight
follows his twisted path and his straight lane

this man's feet hurt, in miserable pain
his shoulders knotted with fatigue
this man is dancing every step
as long and dark as winter nights

it's been an hour since the last streetcar
the man measures how far he's come
by what remains of the soles of his shoes
he's walking this street all night

his lover a none too respectable girl
waits by the river nibbling on nothing
her time is kept by her voracious room
which now is lodging the streetcar man

with eyes half open in the morning light
he flees toward the noisy streetcar stop
and as his beauty sleeps on in her bed
he sighs how sweet it is to feel such love

LES JOUEURS DE MANILLE

La nuit tombera sur ces toits enfouissant ce monde
où nous avons vécu si tranquilles si gais
la catastrophe a toujours été si près de nous que
cette nuit tombe sur ces toits hérissés de tuyaux
ces maisons qui crachent vers le ciel
Que penser de notre vie si tranquille si gaie
si près de cette catastrophe qui devra qui devait
qui doit amener la nuit sur ces toits
si sales que c'en serait à pleurer et que
s'ils pleurent ces toits c'est de la boue qui coule
le long de la bâtisse sur le dos de la foule
s'elles pleurent ces bâtisses ce sont dégorgements
vers les égouts et les cheminées dégorgements et
déjections
vers la terre et vers le ciel leurs déjections
vers la lumière et vers la ténèbre leurs déjections
leurs éjections
déjections de notre vie si tranquille et si gaie
elle en avait l'air
de notre vie si près de la catastrophe que nous
attendons
que nous attendons de cette nuit enfouissant ce monde
bêche la nuit bêche la terre
pour jeter ce monde dans les ténèbres et ses déjections
déjections de notre votre leur vie si tranquille et si gaie
ah manille ah manille
de notre votre leur vie si tranquille et si gaie
ah manille manille *coinchée*

(1935)

THE MANILLE PLAYERS

Night will fall on these roofs that blanket the world
where we've been living so happy so calm
catastrophe has always been so close that
this night is falling on these roofs studded with pipes
these houses spitting at the sky
what are we to think of our lives so happy so calm
so close to this catastrophe which will have to which
had to
which has to bring the night down on these roofs
dirty enough to make them cry and that
if they do then mud would slide
down the walls onto people's backs
if they cry these walls are overflowing
toward sewers and chimneys floods and dejections
toward the earth and toward the sky their dejections
toward light and toward dark their dejections
their ejections
dejections of our lives so happy and so calm
they had the air
of our lives so close to the catastrophe we're waiting
for
that we expect from this night blanketing this world
digging night digging earth
to throw this world into darkness and its dejections
dejections of our your their lives so happy and so calm
oh manille manille
of our your their lives so happy so calm
oh manille manille *coinchée*

RENFORT I

Je vous dis adieu monsieur mon sergent
qui vous en allez à la guerre
vous en aurez pour votre argent
moi je reste avec les mémères
et les vieux de la der des der
qui furent nommés adjudants
et qui au jour de maintenant
sont absolument en retraite
je vous dis adieu monsieur mon sergent
je ne connais que la défaite

REINFORCEMENTS I

My sergeant sir I'm telling you goodbye
as you head off to war
you'll get your money's worth
me I'm staying here with the old grandmas
and the old men from the VFW
who made the grade
and who as of today
are totally retired
My sergeant sir I'm telling you goodbye
all I know is defeat

RENFORT II

Je suis vieux et je suis lourd
mon âge compte on le soupèse
et l'on me dit que vieux et lourd
j'attendrai que la mort me baise
dans un coin—comme un vieux et comme un lourd

REINFORCEMENTS II

I am old and I am heavy
my days are weighed and measured
they tell me that old and heavy
I'll wait for death to screw me
in a corner—like an old man old and heavy

III

Tout est cru, tout est vert, la dent crisse sur l'os
l'émail est agacé par le suc des citrons
le sang coule d'un nez écrasé—une rose
au centre d'une gueule hurlant des abjections
c'est la mort, le supplice—un homme qui transpire
dégagé de sa peau comme un fruit de passion
le bois suinte des cris, le fer coud des tortures
— adieu adieu ma vie, adieu mes horizons
adieu ô mes amours adieu donc ô tendresse
adieux à l'habitude adieux à la maison
adieux à l'espérance à toutes les promesses
— les raisins sont amers et trop verts les citrons
ce n'est plus qu'un tas d'os dont les chiens se
pourlèchent

Everything's raw, everything's green, a tooth cracking
    on a bone
enamel worn away by lemon juice
blood pouring from a broken nose—a rose
in the black hole of a mouth spewing insults
it's death, torture—a sweaty man
slipping out of his skin like a mango
wailing wood dripping, sharp iron knitting
—goodbye goodbye my life, goodbye my horizons
goodbye oh my loves, so goodbye oh tenderness
goodbye habits goodbye home
goodbye hope promises goodbye
—the grapes are sour and the lemons green
all that's left is a pile of bones for the dogs to lick

La mort a écouté le prêche inconsistant
la morale a prêché emporté par le vent
le prêche de morale écouté par la mort
c'est la mort qui écoute et la mort qui entend
l'autre parle sans cesse et sa voix ne demeure
que l'espace d'un souffle emporté par le vent
qui écoute et entend muette et reniflant
l'odeur de ce bon prêche au-dessus de mon temps
c'est mon prêche et ma mort ma morale et mon temps
mon odeur encrassée odeur d'agonisant
car chaque jour je meurs et je prie inconstant
la mort de ma morale emportée à tout vent

The half-baked sermon was heard by death
gone with the wind was the moral preached
the moral's sermon to which death listened
death was listening and death could hear
the other blabbing and his voice resounding
the space of a breath gone with the wind
listening and hearing silent and sniffing
the smell of this sermon too good for my time
my sermon and my death and my moral and my time
sickening stench of my stinking death
my pitifully praying daily death
death of my moral gone with the wind

Sourde est la nuit l'ombre la brume
Sourd est l'arbre sourd le caillou
Sourd est le marteau sur l'enclume
Sourde est la mer sourd le hibou

Aveugles la nuit et la pierre
Aveugles l'herbe et les épis
Aveugle est la taupe sous terre
Aveugle un noyau dans le fruit

Muettes la nuit et la misère
Muets sont les chants et la prairie
Muette est la clarté de l'air
Muet le bois le lac le cri

Infirme est toute la nature
Infirmes sont bêtes et rocs
Infirme est la caricature
Infirme l'idiot qui débloque

Mais qui voit? qui entend? qui parle?

Deaf is the night the shadow the fog
Deaf is the tree deaf the pebble
Deaf is the hammer on the anvil
Deaf is the sea deaf the owl

Blind the night and the stone
Blind the grass and the grain
Blind is the mole under the ground
Blind the kernel inside the fruit

Mute the night and misery
Mute are the songs and the plain
Mute is the air's clarity
Mute the forest the lake the cry

Crippled is all of nature
Crippled are rocks and creatures
Crippled is the caricature
Crippled the idiot healed

But who sees? Who hears? Who speaks?

Calme est l'arbre qui se dresse droit ou bien torve
Calme est aussi l'arbuste en sa médiocrité
Calme est le fier cheval indemne de la morve
Calme est le champignon et sa femme la mousse
Calme est le ruisselet calme aussi le torrent
Calme est le cours fixé qui m'emporte du Temps
Calme la fleur qui meurt Calme l'herbe qui pousse

Calm is the tree standing straight or twisted
Calm too is the bush in its mediocrity
Calm is the proud horse untouched by froth
Calm is the mushroom and its wife the moss
Calm is the little spring calm the torrent too
Calm is the set course removing me from Time
Calm the dying flower Calm the growing grass

Misère de ma vie et vie ô ma misère
misère ô ma vie et misère de vie
quelle ombre quels sujets de cette vie amère
vie oh misère amère, oh misère de vie
une ombre est cette vie et seule la misère
est solide et sans ombre un cristal de lumière
lumière de misère et lumière la vie
oh ma vie oh lumière amère quels sujets
de raison donneront à la vie un cercle de misère
de misère solide comme un cristal d'été
misère des étés misère de la vie
l'ombre m'apportera la misère dernière
ce sera la victoire et la force et la vie
misère de ma vie et vie ô ma misère

Misery of my life and oh my miserable life
misery oh my life and life of misery
what darkness what subjects of this bitter life
life oh bitter misery, oh life of misery
darkness is this life and only misery
is solid and shadowless a crystal of light
light of misery and light of life
oh my life oh bitter light what subjects
of reason will give life a circle of misery
of strong misery like a summer crystal
misery of summers misery of life
darkness will bring me the last misery
it will be victory and strength and life
misery of my life and oh my miserable life

Des jours se sont passés accompagnés de nuits
des jours se sont passés longs de tout un parcours
circulaire longs d'un grand soupir de soleil
d'un aspir hors du sol quand sorti de la mer
il s'égoutte huileux dans la sèche clarté
des jours se sont passés brèves inspirations
que mesurent à peine une épaisseur de feuille
un souvenir ancien sur un calendrier
des jours se sont passés accompagnés des nuits
des nuits longues d'un long sommeil de jour fondu
sous l'horizon gelé veillé par les étoiles
longues comme l'espace et longues comme un temps
Des jours se sont passés accompagnés des nuits
nuits brèves un cri un spasme un heurt
lorsque saute un lapin fusillé dans les bois
des jours se sont passés accompagnés des nuits
et puis c'est tout et ce n'est rien
des jours se sont passés

Days have gone by accompanied by nights
days have gone by with a whole circular
trajectory of a great sigh of sunlight
with the land's breath breathed as it leaves the sea
dripping oily drops in the dry brightness
days have gone by in bursts of inspiration
no deeper than the thickness of a leaf
an ancient memory on a calendar
days have gone by accompanied by nights
long nights of long sleep full of melted days
under the frozen horizon guarded by stars
as long as space and long as a time
Days have gone by accompanied by nights
short nights a cry a spasm a quick crash
when a shot rabbit springs out of the bush
days have gone by accompanied by nights
and well that's all there is and it is nothing
        days have gone by

La lumière poursuit un choc jusqu'en la nuit
de petits yeux éclairs de l'animal nocturne
dont le poil électrique est couché par le vent
regardent hésitants vers un ciel sillonné
par le désir extrême agacé par les nuits
lumières dans la nuit les chocs de la lumière

Light chases a jolt far into the dark
little lightning eyes of the nocturnal beast
whose electric fur is stroked by the wind
shyly watch a sky streaked with
raw desire nights exacerbate
lights in the night jolts of light

L'ombre affiche le fer couvert de rouille et d'os
la faux où suspendu flotte encore un squelette
dans un coin près du feu cuit un œuf à la coque
le crâne qui conçut le sablier du temps

The shadow reveals a bony rusty tool
a skeleton still hanging from the scythe
in a corner by the fire where an egg is boiling
skull that dreamed up the hourglass

Sage renard aux yeux subtils
serpent certain herbes fertiles
atouts des fleurs dans la prairie
l'oiseau filant entre les branches
le soleil dur l'eau qui sourit
la poule qui secoua ses manches . . .

. . . .

. . . les plumes volent ô subtil
renard que le piège agile
pique: puis l'herbe qui s'écarte
recueille les sangs mélangés
de l'oiselle au col écarlate
et du chasseur assassiné!

Such a wise fox with subtle eyes
a certain serpent fertile grass
flowers fanned out across the plain
bird darting through shrubs
smiling water burning sun
hen shaking its cuffs . . .

. . . .

. . . feathers in the air oh subtle
fox fooled by the quick
trap: then the grass spreads
to soak up the mixed blood
of the red-throated bird
and the slain hunter!

Ombre descendue
ombre départ et tristesse
ombre malvenue
ombre espoir et caprice
ombre sur la mer de sérénité
ombre portée au pied des pics
ombre le temps déconcerté
ombre coulant le long des rocs
ombre est l'heure déterminée
ombre est l'ennui après le choc
ombre est l'amour abandonné
ombre la vie ombre la mort
ombre le jour qui t'a vu né
ombre la nuit qui te voit mort
ombre le jour ombre la nuit
ombre la nuit ombre le jour
ombre est l'ombre de toujours
ombre est tout être qui s'enfuit

Shadow lengthening
shadow departure and sorrow
shadow unwelcome
shadow hope and caprice
shadow on the smooth sea
shadow falling at the foot of cliffs
shadow confusing time
shadow flowing alongside rocks
shadow is the predestined hour
shadow is the suffering after a shock
shadow is abandoned love
shadow life shadow death
shadow the day of your birth
shadow the night of your death
shadow day shadow night
shadow night shadow day
shadow is the shadow of always
shadow is all beings slipping away

IV

L'EXPLICATION DES MÉTAPHORES

Loin du temps, de l'espace, un homme est égaré,
Mince comme un cheveu, ample comme l'aurore,
Les naseaux écumants, les deux yeux révulsés,
Et les mains en avant pour tâter le décor

— D'ailleurs inexistant. Mais quelle est, dira-t-on,
La signification de cette métaphore:
« Mince comme un cheveu, ample comme l'aurore »
Et pourquoi ces naseaux hors des trois dimensions?

Si je parle du temps, c'est qu'il n'est pas encore,
Si je parle d'un lieu, c'est qu'il a disparu,
Si je parle d'un homme, il sera bientôt mort,
Si je parle du temps, c'est qu'il n'est déjà plus,

Si je parle d'espace, un dieu vient le détruire,
Si je parle des ans, c'est pour anéantir,
Si j'entends le silence, un dieu vient y mugir
Et ses cris répétés ne peuvent que me nuire.

Car ces dieux sont démons; ils rampent dans l'espace,
Minces comme un cheveu, amples comme l'aurore,
Les naseaux écumants, la bave sur la face,
Et les mains en avant pour saisir un décor

—D'ailleurs inexistant. Mais quelle est, dira-t-on,
La signification de cette métaphore
« Minces comme un cheveu, amples comme l'aurore »
Et pourquoi cette face hors des trois dimensions?

THE EXPLANATION OF METAPHORS

Outside of time and space, a man is lost
Thin as a hair, wide as the light of dawn,
Foam in his nostrils, eyes bulging aghast,
And hands reaching out in search of the scene

—Unreal in fact. So, one will likely ask,
What is the meaning of this metaphor:
"Thin as a hair, wide as the light of dawn"
And why these less than three-dimensional nostrils?

If I should speak of time, it hasn't happened,
If I should speak of a place, it's disappeared,
If I should speak of a man, he'll soon be dead,
If I should speak of time, it's come and gone.

If I should speak of space, a god's destroyed it,
If I should speak of years, it's to erase them,
If I hear silence, a god comes roaring through it,
And his repeated cries give me great grief.

Because these gods are demons; they crawl through
space,
Thin as a hair, wide as the light of dawn,
Foam in their nostrils, slobber on their face,
And hands reaching out in search of the scene

—Unreal in fact. So, one will likely ask,
What is the meaning of this metaphor:
"Thin as a hair, wide as the light of dawn"
And why this less than three-dimensional face?

Si je parle des dieux, c'est qu'ils couvrent la mer
De leur poids infini, de leur vol immortel,
Si je parle des dieux, c'est qu'ils hantent les airs,
Si je parle des dieux, c'est qu'ils sont perpétuels,

Si je parle des dieux, c'est qu'ils vivent sous terre,
Insufflant dans le sol leur haleine vivace,
Si je parle des dieux, c'est qu'ils couvent le fer,
Amassent le charbon, distillent le cinabre.

Sont-ils dieux ou démons? Ils emplissent le temps,
Minces comme un cheveu, amples comme l'aurore,
L'émail des yeux brisés, les naseaux écumants,
Et les mains en avant pour saisir un décor

—D'ailleurs inexistant. Mais quelle est, dira-t-on,
La signification de cette métaphore
« Mince comme un cheveu, ample comme une aurore »
Et pourquoi ces deux mains hors des trois dimensions?

Oui, ce sont des démons. L'un descend, l'autre monte.
A chaque nuit son jour, à chaque mont son val,
A chaque jour sa nuit, à chaque arbre son ombre,
A chaque être son Non, à chaque bien son mal,

Oui, ce sont des reflets, images négatives,
S'agitant à l'instar de l'immobilité,
Jetant dans le néant leur multitude active
Et composant un double à toute vérité.

Mais ni dieu ni démon l'homme s'est égaré,
Mince comme un cheveu, ample comme l'aurore,
Les naseaux écumants, les deux yeux révulsés,
Et les mains en avant pour tâter un décor

If I should speak of gods, they span the sea,
With their infinite weight, their perpetual flight,
If I should speak of gods, they haunt the air,
If I should speak of gods, they never die,

If I should speak of gods, they're underground,
Breathing their vital breath into the soil
If I should speak of gods, they nurture iron,
They gather carbon and distill cinnabar.

So, are they gods or demons? They fill time
Thin as a hair, wide as the light of dawn,
Foam in their nostrils, hollow enamel eyes,
And hands reaching out in search of the scene

—Unreal in fact. So, one will likely ask,
What is the meaning of this metaphor:
"Thin as a hair, wide as the light of dawn"
And why these less than three-dimensional hands?

Yes, they are demons. One goes down, one up.
A day for every night, a valley for every hill,
A night for every day, a shadow for every tree,
A No for every being, an evil for every good,

Yes, they're reflections, negative images,
Moving about like immobility,
Hurling their many selves into the void
And creating a double for every truth.

But neither god nor demon, man is lost,
Thin as a hair, wide as the light of dawn,
Foam in his nostrils, eyes bulging aghast,
And hands reaching out in search of the scene

—D'ailleurs inexistant. C'est qu'il est égaré;
Il n'est pas assez mince, il n'est pas assez ample:
Trop de muscles tordus, trop de salive usée.
Le calme reviendra lorsqu'il verra le Temple
De sa forme assurer sa propre éternité.

—Unreal in fact. For he is truly lost;
He isn't thin enough, nor wide enough:
Too many muscles flexed, saliva swallowed.
Calm will return when he sees the Temple
Secure in form its own eternity.

CYGNES

Quand Un fit l'amour avec Zéro
Les sphères embrassèrent les tores
Et les nombres premiers s'avancèrent
Tendant leurs mains vers les frais sycomores
Et les fractions continues blessées à mort
Dans le torrent des décimales muettes se couchèrent

Quand B fit l'amour avec A
Les paragraphes s'embrasèrent
Les virgules s'avancèrent
Tendant leur cou par-dessus les ponts de fer
Et l'alphabet blessé za mort
S'évanouit dans les bras d'une interrogation muette

SWAN-SIGNS

When One made love with Zero
Spheres embraced the torus
Prime numbers stepped forward
Their hands reaching for fresh sycamore
And simple fractions mortally wounded
Lay down in the torrent of mute decimals

When B made love with A
Paragraphs embraced blushing
Commas stepped forward
Stretching their necks over the iron bridges
And the alphabet mortally wounded
Collapsed in the arms of a mute question mark

MAGIE NOIRE

Profitant de la nuit voici le sale prophète
Empruntant un noir chemin où seul se promène
Fleuve embourbant les bois où nulle nulle fleur
Flamine embarbouillé de foie avec nulle nulle flamme

Prétexte que le soir lisant texte après texte
S'apprêtait à la solitude où lui inverse prêtre
Flânait terrifiant les démons et narguant les effluves
Flavescentes triviales en enfer où dénigrantes et
flambantes

Proue du destin mauvais malheur infect qui s'apprête
Prétendant dire les maux mais ignare du présent
Pourpre banalité vers les mots qu'il prononce

Fluide phonétique faux sons du guignon l'oriflamme
Flattant qui sourd néfaste orgueilleux de son flegme
Flétrisseur bonhomme il paraît à tout moment flébile

BLACK MAGIC

Exploiting the darkness the dirty prophet
Taking a black road walked by no one else
A river muddying woods where no no flower
Flimmers muddily as liver with no no flame

The night's pretext perusing text after text
The perverted priest prepared for solitude where
He strutted scaring off demons and taunting fumes
Petty fluvescent hellbent spited flamed

Destiny's prow lousy disgusting luck
Ready to fake badmouthing the absent present
Purple banalities toward the words he speaks

Fluid phonetic false notes luckless flag
Flattering flowing full of his own phlegm
Self-flaunting fellow forever so flebile

MAGIE BLANCHE

Ces serpents qui jaillissent hors de cette serviette
Ce sont quatre foulards que jeta ce sorcier
Si vous saviez amis ce que vaut sa
Science vous ririez abattus par trop de scepticisme

Tonnez canons de cuivre! sur la corde tirez!
Tracez cercles de feu, fusées, pissat d'étoiles!
Travaillez par dur labeur douces colombes qui tombez
Tendres et blanches neiges hors du filet attrape

Dans tous les gobelets sont liquides ou dés
Dés mépris du calcul liqueur chimie des diables
Déroute de la vue des cinq sens dérision

Dans la poche profonde se cache sa défense
Travailleur syndiqué en frac Noël des jours d'étrenne
Ce savant qui déçoit artiste qui se sauve

WHITE MAGIC

These snakes springing from this handkerchief
The magician makes appear are four long scarves
This tricky science friends if only you knew
The way it's done you'd die of disbelief

Blow copper cannons! Shoot straight ahead!
Blast off your fireworks, make the stars piss!
Bust your falling asses lily-white doves
Blip through the net as soft as snow

Drinks and dice are dripping into cups
Dice scorn of strategy booze devils' chemistry
Derailed vision all five senses duped

Tuxedoed union worker gifted Christmas
Buried deep in his pocket his defense
Deceitful scholar artist who flees the scene

CREVASSE

Du crâne qui crugit lorsque le vent souffle
suinte mélancolicolicoliquement
le croupissant cresson qui sourd de ses orbites

Crions! crions! toujours bêle l'os armature
et gémit mélodieulodieusement
le croisé des crocs qui scient un peu d'espace

Telle crevasse en la cronfusion quotidienne
crécelle le sourire et creuse le bonheur
        mais

qui tire la langue an crétin croquemitaine?
cré nom! crois-je bien que c'est moi

CREVASSE

Wind is blowing through the wroaring skull
in such a melancholycholycholy way
that wrotten watercress broozes out of its eyebrawls

Holy baloney! The retrofit bone's still bleating
and moaning melodioulodiously
the crossed fangs sawing a little space

Such a crevasse in the quotidian cronfusion
creaseals the smile and crashes happiness
        but

who sticks his tongue out at the idiot ogre?
Wesus! I wink it's me

LES ZIAUX

les eaux bruns, les eaux noirs, les eaux de merveille
les eaux de mer, d'océan, les eaux d'étincelles
nuitent le jour, jurent la nuit
chants de dimanche à samedi

les yeux vertes, les yeux bleues, les yeux de succelle
les yeux de passante au cours de la vie
les yeux noires, yeux d'estanchelle
silencent les mots, ouatent le bruit

eau de ces yeux penché sur tout miroir
gouttes secrets au bord des veilles
tout miroir, toute veille en ces ziaux bleues ou vertes
les ziaux bruns, les ziaux noirs, les ziaux de merveille

(1943)

EYESEAS

brownwaters, blackwaters, wonderwaters
seawaters, oceanwaters, flashingwaters
brighten the night, nighten the day
songs Sunday to Saturday

green eyes, blue eyes, juicesipping eyes
eyes of a woman glanced in passing
her black eyes, her lakerippling eyes
silence the words, muffle the noise

seas of these eyes over every mirror
teardrops secrets at the edge of sleeplessness
all mirrors, all sleeplessness in these blue or green
eyeseas
brown eyeseas, black eyeseas, wonder eyeseas

1943